#'S Aren't Enough!

A GIRLFRIEND'S GUIDE TO SHOWING UP AND CONQUERING THE LEADERSHIP CRISIS

SHELLEY DUNAGAN

COOPERTUCKER PRESS

Hashtags Aren't Enough: A Girlfriend's Guide to Showing Up and Conquering the Leadership Crisis

Published by CooperTucker Press.

Disclaimer

ISBN: 978-0-578-46705-4

DEDICATION

To Julie, Cooper, and Tucker: You are my world. I love you!

ACKNOWLEDGMENTS

I would like to thank my parents, Pat and Cindy Dunagan, for helping to instill my confidence, and my siblings Lisa and Dean Dunagan for fueling my competitiveness. Thank you to my family and my friends who are family for your constant support, enthusiasm, and coaching; and my clients and colleagues who continue to teach me something new every day along this journey.

Contents

INTRODUCTION

A NEWS ALERT ABOUT a bill in California blew my mind the other day. As of 2019, all publicly listed companies headquartered in the state must have at least one woman on their boards.

I did a *double* take as I looked at my phone when I first saw this headline, for we're not in the Victorian era, after all. Is it to make a law specifically addressing gender equity in organizations?

Damn skippy it is!

In spite of the research out there that reinforces the correlation between women in leadership and accelerated corporate performance (Thompson Reuters, Credit Suisse, and McKinsey, for starters), a global female leadership crisis remains. Today. Right now! There are over **600 public companies** with revenues in the billions that do not have any female directors on their boards.

There might be a token female Human Resources leader, maybe a female corporate attorney, a Chief Financial Officer if you're lucky, so perhaps some female representation somewhere within the senior management ranks. But you get where I'm going. I have worked with companies that do not have a single woman in their senior leadership team. If I had a dollar for every executive

I've worked with who's said, "We don't have many women on our board," I'd be able to retire early.

Even when women do manage to obtain leadership roles, it's often an uphill battle for them to succeed and find longevity in those positions. In the last year alone, we saw the departure of women from chief executive roles in companies such as PepsiCo, Mattel, and Avon— and all of those roles have been refilled by men. Research shows that female executives also are more likely to be put in charge of firms that are already in crisis — setting women up for failure.

The reality is that people like to hire and collaborate with individuals who they can relate to and see in themselves. So, you can imagine where the issue lies when companies have boards, hiring managers, recruitment specialists, and senior management who are all men. Women are seen as "the other," or as people who "just won't mesh well with our company's culture" [read: our old boys club].

The homogeneity of many corporate workplaces impacts women's experiences on all levels. Where a male co-worker might have no problem finding mentors and role models he can relate to, it may be slim pickings for a woman in the same company.

On top of the sheer lack of women in leadership roles who could act as mentors, some men are avoiding their female colleagues altogether in light of the increased attention being paid to sexual harassment in the wake of the #MeToo movement. When straight-up avoidance of women in the workplace becomes the norm, how are we supposed to have access to the same opportunities as our male co-workers? How can we schmooze clients, build our networks, work our professional contacts, and showcase our skills if half the people in the room won't even acknowledge us?

This avoidance sets up the workplace to produce the unbalanced hiring practices, unequal pay, and lack of professional opportunities women encounter today. Also , women have the added stress of being expected to maintain roles now ingrained into societal norms. The mother, the household manager, the planner, the organizer, the caregiver — these are all time-consuming and emotional roles that fight for our concentration and focus.

If we drop any of the countless balls we have in the air, the rest of the world is quick to let us know exactly how miserably we've failed. Men, on the other hand, are praised for showing up at school sporting events, for getting home for dinner, for remembering an essential personal date, or for spending time with the kids.

Women are expected to do all of those things and more with little to no recognition, and we are often put in a position where we're damned if we do and damned if we don't. If we stay late at the office to finish compiling a report, we're neglectful and selfish mothers; conversely, if we leave the office on time to go home to our family, we're told that we don't have the ambition to succeed in a leadership role.

My view from inside

There are no quick fixes to the barriers and problems we face today, and that's part of why I decided to write this book. Now more than ever, we must figure out how we can challenge the status quo in all of its forms. In my 20+ years of working with numerous companies, I've tried countless strategies, and I can tell you that the same old song and dance aren't going to cut it anymore.

I spent years joking, "Not a lot of estrogen in this conference room." It was always a delicate balancing act between not staying silent and not coming across as too aggressive. The irony in me having to soften my approach to supposedly cut-throat, tough CEOs wasn't lost on me, but hey— whatever works!

As a Leadership Effectiveness and Revenue Acceleration Guru, I've been able to test out new approaches to creating more opportunities for women in leadership. If you're thinking to yourself, *What in the heck does that job title even mean*, I'm a corporate fixer. Think Olivia Pope, but with marginally less violence and conspiracy!

Make no mistake, though; my life might not look exactly like Olivia Pope's, but tears have still been shed, gladiators have been rallied, and we've won some wars.

I have gained my knowledge and experience rising to top leadership roles in my sales profession and then taking on consulting gigs for companies ranging in revenue from 10 million to 3 billion dollars. I have helped them attract top talent, complete strategic plans, compensation plans, and accountability metrics, as well as guided them through significant change initiatives.

In some cases, I was successful in pushing organizations to diversify their leadership team. They might hire a woman to be the VP of Sales or a VP of Marketing, and then promptly make her the go-to person for all diversity-related questions. But that was usually as high up the ladder as they would go.

These days, I am an executive coach who also holds four Leadership Accelerators throughout the country for just 32 leaders or emerging leaders. There is very little I haven't seen or successfully participated in.

I want to bring these experiences to life for you and leave you with a roadmap for your journey.

3 things smart women can do to accelerate their leadership track

I was reminiscing about some of those prior battles when I first started thinking about writing this book. A quote I'd heard from Oprah Winfrey popped into my head and described my thoughts perfectly:

"It's time to step out of the history that is holding you back and step into the new story you are willing to create."

Are you a smart, capable, qualified woman? Do you feel stuck as to how you can move forward in your career and become the badass leader you know you can be?

If so, let's talk about overcoming the barriers in your path and how to accelerate your leadership journey. We need new strategies if we want to create a new story, and that's what I'm hoping you'll get out of this book.

I've compiled the lessons I've learned (some of them the hard way) to try to help us keep from repeating the past. Whether you're a senior executive or a coach, a teacher or a college student, this book is for you. I've written it as a sort of playbook that you can reference no matter where you're at in your career, complete with all the tools you need to succeed as a female leader.

Throughout my years as a Leadership Effectiveness Guru and Executive Coach, I've had the privilege of mentoring women who aspire to become leaders in their chosen careers. Many of these women have felt stuck. They had the qualifications and the drive to lead, but they didn't know how to become that leader.

I always tell them that the red carpet to leadership is rarely rolled out in front of you. Heck, if you're a woman, the red carpet is also littered with potholes and road kill. But do not despair! I have three steps that can accelerate you on your track to leadership this year.

The three steps are:

1. **Know** your worth to the organization and advocate for yourself.
2. **Focus** on the overall health of your organization.
3. **Embrace and evangelize** the upside of *disruption* in your organization.

In the next few sections, I'll go into more detail about these steps so that YOU can start down your accelerated path to leadership.

If you're ready to stop living in the past and create your own future, then read on — let's see what we can collectively do to write our stories as female leaders!

I want to be the queen.

STEP ONE: KNOW YOUR WORTH AND BECOME YOUR OWN ADVOCATE

"Dreams and reality are opposites.
Action synthesizes them."

— Assata Shakur

WHAT ARE THREE things that make you unique?

On the road to leadership, you must first have an understanding of your worth to an organization. Ask yourself what it is about YOU that makes you an asset to your organization.

Are you a genius with computers? Do you have a knack for leading group projects? Are you the most consistent performer and have the data to prove it? Maybe you are the queen of special projects, always going above and beyond your duties. Or, perhaps your energy and dedication inspire everyone around you.

If you don't know what makes you an exceptional employee, you won't be able to tell your bosses why you deserve that promotion instead of Bob, the intern.

What are *YOUR three unique qualities?* Write them down.

"No one is you, and that is your power."

– Dave Grohl

Once you've identified three unique traits about yourself and have assembled the data and specific track record to back it all up, you must become your advocate. Vocalize your strengths whenever the appropriate opportunity arises.

I don't mean that you should spout them off willy-nilly, like when you're sitting next to your boss in a critical stakeholder meeting, or strangers on the subway. Think performance reviews, interviews, or when a co-worker needs help with a particular activity that your unique quality serves.

My father would brag to his friends about every little thing I did when I was a small tyke, from good grades to playing a tree stump in the elementary school play. You must be your proud dad. **<u>Be your advocate.</u>**

I am one of the few people who looks hot eating a cupcake.

Ask your boss for validation and a strategy to get to the next level

As your advocate, performance reviews provide an opportunity for you to share your unique traits with your boss. These reviews are also a time to get validation from your boss about all the great things you offer the company.

If your organization doesn't do regular performance reviews, ask your employer to start. Sell them on the fact that what gets measured gets done. High-performing organizations all know how to get the most out of performance reviews.

But don't stop there, because awareness of your abilities must not stop with just your immediate supervisor. And one reason highly talented people don't get promoted has nothing to do with them; it may have everything to do with the insecurity of their direct supervisor or boss.

This supervisor may have an unconscious fear that someone will take their job. Possibly, this person doesn't have the power to promote you. Perhaps, this person routinely promotes men over women. Maybe, just maybe, this person only wants to promote family members, like an alcoholic uncle with a gambling addiction. You never know.

If your boss doesn't do performance reviews, take a deep breath, a leap of faith, and set up a meeting with your boss's boss. You will look like a badass. If you have confidence in your three unique qualities, and what you bring to the table, this is your opportunity to show that you have "high potential."

It may be one of the most satisfying meetings you will have in your career. Take this opportunity to ask them how you can strategically get to the next level. Are there other key leaders in the organization they could recommend you learn from?

Make a plan

Taking the initiative to set up a meeting with your boss, or your boss's boss is one of the best ways for you to advocate for what comes next. But you must approach this meeting with clear goals and must seek more than just reassurance.

During your meeting, tell your employer about your aspirations and make a plan together. Agree on goals and time frames needed to achieve your move to the next level in the company. Decide on a specific date for your next promotion. **You and your boss are building a strategy for your track to leadership.**

Before the meeting ends, set up the next meeting to review your progress. If your organization does annual reviews, consider asking for quarterly reviews. You are ultimately responsible for your climb up the ladder, so stay focused on your three unique qualities and your strategic goals.

All I need to do is focus and stay calm.

Ask your peers for validation

You should not only share your aspirations with your employer, you should share them with your peers as well. They are an excellent source for a reality check and can often provide valuable insight into how to improve your standing and workplace profile.

We all need an outside eye to show us things about ourselves that we may not be aware of, both positive and negative. Ask them whether they think you would be a successful leader. Ask them what you should focus on and where you can improve.

Some of the most noteworthy advice I received throughout my career came from my peers. Guidance that I got from a peer proved to be career-making when I was just three years into the workforce.

At the time, I was a successful sales representative working for Sprint. I wanted to go into management and was starting to make this known. I was quite full of myself at the time and felt entitled to a management position because I had exceeded my sales numbers and had just won a company-sponsored contest for a presentation on how to teach people about a complex new product offering.

One of my peers suggested that, if I wanted to advance in the company, I should join the training department, since I already had their attention after winning the contest. It was absolutely an "aha" moment. I took my peer's advice and joined the training team. It worked better than anticipated, and I became a sales leader within 18 months.

I have often credited that early move in my career to all the successes that followed. If it wasn't for a peer pointing out to me that I had an opportunity to capitalize on a unique talent for training people, I might not have moved up the ladder so quickly.

Your peers can also give you insight into the current leadership that you may not have noticed. Maybe one of your peers knows your boss personally. Perhaps they have experienced the good and bad of their leadership style. All of this information can be invaluable in helping you to smartly approach your boss when you want to form your advancement strategy.

Don't be afraid to put yourself out there. It's easy to fall into thinking that nobody will care about your leadership aspirations, but there are people out there who will help you.

How can I get access to more professional development?

One common question I get from people who are trying to expand their leadership skills is how can they get support from their organization to take part in professional development opportunities.

Professional development is an investment in you and what you can bring to the company. The more you learn, the more value you have to the organization. But don't wait for that invitation.

The first rule is to always ask; your supervisor or board might turn you down, but they also might surprise you and say yes. Don't be shy about asking for the company to help cover monetary expenses, too.

Your performance review or your discussion with your supervisor's boss would be a great place to get this discussion going — and to gain commitments with specific timetables attached.

Also, consider working to build professional development opportunities into your organization. This might entail each employee being given a set professional development fund each year, having a pool of funds for the office that individuals can request to use or setting up another process that makes sense for your organization.

Here is a sample request template that I provide to folks who want to attend one of the quarterly "Dig Deeper" Leadership Accelerators I host. A similar request can be used for any development opportunity:

Sample Professional Development Request

Dear (Insert Manager's Name):

I would like your approval to attend a two day "Dig Deeper" Leadership Accelerator. It takes place on (insert dates) at (insert location). I have done my research and the biggest difference between the "Dig Deeper" Accelerator and other conferences is that this is a hands-on, completely immersive, working session limited to 32 leaders from across the country.

As a group, we will share our own best practices as well as learn the best practices implemented for numerous organizations by The Dunagan Group to tackle the ever-changing role of successful leadership. I will receive a year's worth of customized leadership coaching in just two days that I can bring back and apply to our organization.

Here are some of the agenda sessions that I will benefit from:

- Creating high-performance, thriving teams
- Embracing disruption to accelerate performance
- The "best of" employee engagement strategies
- Accountability that motivates
- Recruiting and assessing top talent

By attending this accelerator, I will be able to step away from the day-to-day focus of being in the business and focus on my approach, strategy, mindset, and skills. I will leave with a new toolbox that I can start using immediately.

Here is the approximate cost breakdown for me to attend:

- Airfare $<insert amount>
- Hotel $<insert amount>
- Accelerator $<insert amount> *List any early bird discount with date

Upon my return, I will share key takeaways, including those we can implement immediately to accelerate our success.

I would greatly appreciate your approval and investment in me. If you have any questions about the accelerator, please let me know.

Best Regards,

XXX

Again, one of the primary things to keep in mind is clearly connecting the value your professional development will bring to the whole organization.

To summarize step one on your track to leadership:

- Start out by understanding your worth and what you uniquely contribute to the organization.

- Then advocate for yourself by letting your boss (and boss's boss) know your value. Make a plan with your employer about how you will move toward the leadership role you desire and deserve.

- And finally, ask your peers for an honest evaluation of strengths and weaknesses. Glean information from them about your work that might help you navigate your road to success.

STEP TWO: Focus on the Health
of the Organization

"You can focus on things that are barriers or you can focus on scaling the wall or redefining the problem."

—Tim Cook

IF YOUR ORGANIZATION isn't healthy, there will be fewer opportunities to advance. Even if a single sector or department of the organization is sick, the rest of the company suffers, and your chances of becoming a leader in your company suffer along with it. After all, if you break your leg, the rest of your body isn't going far.

Smart leaders know how to bust down the silos that exist and focus on the overall health of the organization. Want to be a leader? Then you'll have to become a silo-buster. Being a silo buster is like being a super-heroine but without the Spandex (and more pantsuits).

First, let's focus on what I mean when I talk about silos, how they can harm your organization, and how you can potentially tackle them to help advance your career.

Silos emerge as a business grows. When a business first forms, everyone works together. There are usually just a few employees, and each is responsible for multiple jobs. They may hold the title of COO or CMO, but they run IT, Sales, and Customer Satisfaction all at the same time. Silos don't exist because the resources aren't there to support them and the need for specialists hasn't yet arrived.

As a business begins to grow, workload expansion requires that some duties become more separate and new resources are invested in developing specialized capabilities, in hiring, sales or production as examples. Teams are created to support different more specialized functions, and the first silos begin to rise.

Siloing, defined as a verb by Merriam Webster, means to isolate (a core system, process, or department, for example) from others.

With growth, each department in an organization needs to develop and focus on the specific processes, goals, and objectives that will make their contribution to the organization consistent and productive. This is a good thing. However, it can also become a destructive thing for an organization when departments become overly isolated.

If each department builds its silo and puts their systems and processes in place without regard to the operation of the organization as a whole, isolation rears its ugly head, and multiple problems begin to develop. These include (but aren't limited to): disparate systems that don't talk to each other; the silo blame game when things aren't working; and a lack of focus on the overall vision and goals of the organization.

Silos are a critical issue for 95 percent of the organizations with which I work. They are often the root cause of numerous problems that impact growth and performance.

Even the very best leaders often need support and coaching on how to facilitate silo-busting. I coach emerging leaders to look for opportunities within their organizations to break up silos, as it will accelerate their leadership path because of the value it brings to their executive team.

How to approach silos

Today, I begin each of my client engagements by completing an initial assessment of organizational health. I ask for an all-access pass to speak with the leaders of each functional area. If I am not granted this pass, I don't move forward with the engagement.

I didn't always take such a hard-line approach, but I learned the hard way that access and support from leadership teams are vital if I'm going to assess the organization holistically. If I tried to move forward minus those factors, I ended up contributing to a siloed environment and was unable to cultivate long-term success. Each and every time I have been successful with revenue acceleration and performance coaching it is because I was allowed to traverse the silos.

One example of an epic failure to improve a client's performance has stuck with me over the years and forced me to hold firm to the all-access pass. Take note of it as you consider assessing the silos within your organization, and how you might best tackle the dysfunction silos can create.

I was asked to engage with a 150-person software organization to fix their sales numbers. I had several meetings with the CEO during which he consistently articulated that the **sales department** was solely responsible for the organization's lack of growth. We discussed sales rep turnover, lack of prospecting, lack of a robust pipeline, and what he deemed a lack of effective sales leadership.

I encouraged this CEO to tell me more about marketing, service implementation, and the customer's journey through his organization. Rather than expanding the conversation to include these areas, he abruptly told me that all of these other areas were doing great. He asked me to keep my focus and scope on sales. "Help us make them accountable; that is all we need to do," he excitedly proclaimed.

My practice was just getting started — this was only my third gig — so I agreed to work exclusively with sales. I told him I would begin by assessing the skills and performance of his sales leaders and teams.

I was 15 minutes into my first meeting with the key sales stake-holders when I learned about the many ways the rest of the organization was impeding the sales team's success. I like to look at issues as opportunities, and there were several key areas of opportunity that were exposed.

These opportunities for growth included missed software release dates, lack of marketing, the inability of prospects to navigate the website, no CRM to make prospecting and up-selling more productive, and implementation dates that were being pushed out due to numerous "internal issues."

One of my best talents is my ability to cut through the BS and whining and determine what issues are genuinely impacting performance and which are being used as a smokescreen to hide from accountability. As I moved throughout the sales organization, I confirmed that all of the above issues were, in fact, actual barriers to sales success.

Unfortunately, the climate was growing increasingly negative as these issues were not even being taken into consideration by the executive team. The conversations were turning ugly. It was the sales silo vs. all of the other silos, and those still left (50 percent of the sales team deserted the fight and left the company) felt like they were constantly fighting a losing battle.

I heard it all.

"They (operations) can't provide us with a realistic release date."

"Why do we even have a marketing team; they don't even know what we sell?"

You get the idea. Some of you may be shaking your heads in acknowledgment and empathy for these folks. Many of us have been there or are currently experiencing the same thing in our own organizations. For an aspiring leader, all those grinding gears are opportunities to show your stuff.

I gathered all of the relevant data points from my discussions and evaluations and scheduled another meeting with the CEO to discuss the next steps. My goal was to focus the conversation around his customer's journey throughout the organization. I felt that if I could force him to take a deep dive into this journey, some of the non-sales reasons for poor performance would come to light. I stressed several times that a customer's journey is impacted by each employee, leader, and function within the company.

Yes, I was trying to justify and gain approval once again for my all-access pass. I knew that securing his sponsorship to look at the entire organization's performance was my only hope for sustainable performance improvement. I was also confident that if I was given the pass, I could put together a strategy that was exponentially more likely to be successful.

This CEO told me to pump the brakes. He confessed that he knew there were some other problems, but he still believed that if I could give sales better metrics and a more lucrative compensation plan to help retain staff, things would start to turn around.

He also insisted that a lot of the issues raised were just excuses. He told me he hired me because I knew more about running successful sales organizations than he did and to please get moving on it. He believed in his heart that, if we started holding the sales team more accountable, they wouldn't have the time to make excuses.

I am saddened to report that I am not the hero of my own story here. I continued on with the gig and focused my efforts on accountability metrics and the creation of a lucrative compensation plan. I had many reservations, but I forged ahead in spite of them.

The hard reality for me was that, without my all-access pass, I knew I wasn't going to be able to facilitate all of the changes that were needed to accelerate success. I wrote a well-received compensation plan, streamlined the sales process, and developed specific metrics to help the team — all while knowing that it wouldn't be enough.

I said my goodbyes and wished them all well. Today, that company is dying a slow death. Only one salesperson remains from a high of 15, and they have unsuccessfully tried to sell the company on three separate occasions.

So how do you do it?

One lesson from the failed experience I just shared is that notion of the all-access pass, and what having it can provide when you are seeking to identify specific cross-departmental problems to go after. You want that broad overview perspective

The lesson here is an important one for all aspiring leaders to understand. Lack of growth is never due to just one problem, a single part of the organization, one bad leader, or one lost customer. Lack of growth comes from a lack of focus on the overall business and the existence of silos that foster isolated decisions and chaos.

That said, breaking down well-built silos is not an easy endeavor. Long-established behaviors don't just change because we ask people to change them, but strong leaders can get it done.

Breaking out of your silo and bringing your peers together to focus on the things you identify as hindering the overall health of the organization can paint you as a leader and significantly increase your opportunities for advancement.

And don't ask permission to tackle meaningful problems. Author Ayn Rand said, "The question isn't who is going to let me; it's who is going to stop me."

Here's a summary of what you can do to become a silo-buster:

1. Pick three behaviors or systems that are having a negative impact on the entire organization. **Do not try to boil the ocean here.** Even the smallest changes can help the overall health of a company. This can include dealing with low company morale, fixing email communication issues, or making sure everyone is aware of new rules and regulations.

2. Recruit your co-workers and form a cross-departmental peer council that spends 90 minutes a week focusing on ways to improve the three problems you identified. These changes can include creating a newsletter focused on employee success stories, creating universal email signatures for everyone, or starting a SharePoint repository for all important company information.

3. Decide with your peer council how you will advocate for change and communicate the change to the rest of the company.

4. Identify a senior executive who will sponsor your success and join your meetings.

5. Document your success.

6. Make it fun for the team to build engagement! You can design a silly t-shirt together as a team-building project that reads, "We are the silo-busters!"

Let's take a closer look at each of those steps.

Silos exist. How are they impacting growth?

Silos exist in most organizations. Recognize that they exist in yours and understand why. Most are born from immediate necessity. A problem exists, Band-aids are sought out to stop the bleeding, and a process is born that may well have negative impacts outside of the silo.

Take the time to look at all of your organization's Band-aids and understand the impact they are having on overall growth.

Establish a cross-departmental "silo-busting" team

Understanding the impact of silos is a necessary first step, but you have to follow up with a process that will result in a specific and detailed plan of action.

The best way to do that is to recruit a cross-departmental team of 7-9 people whose sole purpose will be to focus on specific goals and issues. They will be responsible for developing an action plan to tackle each of the issues that are identified.

This team should have an executive sponsor that attends all meetings, so you will need to seek out a senior executive who will sponsor your success.

Choose this team wisely. The individuals you select need to be able to challenge the status quo and take action that people will follow. Do not pick a team of "thinkers," as they will never be able to implement the starts and stops necessary.

You want to galvanize these people to take action. One way I often start these teams is by asking them to examine the customer's journey throughout the organization. The customer's journey or experience touches almost every part of the organization, so it is an excellent opportunity to unify teams behind that journey.

From there, I ask them to map out what the ideal journey would look like and identify the challenges that stand in the way of that ideal experience. Addressing those challenges becomes their goal.

Focus them in on these goals and gain agreement on the expected time frame for achievement.

This team should meet once a week for 90 minutes at the same time each week without exception. Make sure the people you select will be 100 percent committed to the effort.

Focus that team on specific goals and set hard time frames for achievement

As an outsider in an organization, I sometimes become a magnet for what I call "true confessions." People don't just talk to me about their frustrations when I ask; they are compelled to seek me out, schedule time on my calendar, and pour their hearts and souls out to me. This is often the result of not being heard by their leaders.

I don't discourage this behavior as it is a necessary part of facilitating change. However, I do end these sessions with specific asks. I ask each individual to tell me one thing that they would start doing immediately if they were in charge. I then ask them to tell me one thing they would stop doing. Depending on their answers, I either ask them to come back to me in a week with a plan outlining what needs to happen to effect that change or I ask them to bring me a list that details who and what will be impacted by the proposed change.

The best leaders are great at doing this. They put a premium on this type of communication, and as a result, they get the most out of their people. I have found that women leaders are especially good at doing this, perhaps because this skill is more societally ingrained in them.

In your silo-busting effort, you are looking to compile the top 3 "starts" and "stops" and put together an action plan to implement them.

In my engagement, 95% of the people who came to me stated that their #1 'start' would be trying to bring their organization together. This organization was so siloed, they had 22 different processes in place just for pricing and placing orders. They came up with actionable ideas to better align departments and streamline processes. That's the kind of thing you need from your council to take to senior management.

Find a way to regularly share the council's progress with the entire organization

Your team cannot exist in a vacuum. Lack of communication kills healthy corporate cultures. When people don't feel heard or when they don't hear from their senior leaders, they become complacent, or worse— they become frustrated. Frustrated teams don't grow revenues!

The best thing you can do to tear down silos is to promote open and honest communication throughout the organization. Ask your council members to talk with their people and encourage them to listen to what is said as they ask for ideas.

Share progress weekly, so everyone is aware of what work is being done. Highlight achievements in emails or newsletters so that others start to rally around the team. You will start to see that more and more people will become invested in the success.

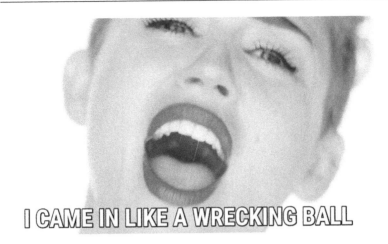

I CAME IN LIKE A WRECKING BALL

In conclusion

Don't get discouraged if you run into opposition while you're trying to bust down silos. Change can be scary, and people are often reluctant to admit that there's a problem in the first place.

If you stick with it, though, the benefits to your organization and your effort to highlight your leadership abilities will be enormous. Keep your eye on the prize and keep working until the silos are dismantled!

STEP THREE: EMBRACE AND EVANGELIZE THE UPSIDE OF DISRUPTION

SIMPLY PUT, THE best leaders know how to embrace disruption in their organization. What exactly are disruptions in an organization? The list is long but think of things like new leadership, new sales tools, any new technological improvements, or a new delivery driver with devastatingly good looks.

I have witnessed first-hand people failing as leaders because they don't embrace disruption. The inability to accept change keeps business practices stagnant. To be an effective leader, you must first be a follower of change. Need some inspiration? Watch Derek Sivers' viral YouTube video "First Follower: Leadership Lessons from Dancing Guy."[1]

In the video, Sivers explains that the way to be an effective leader is to first be a courageous follower. He shows a clip of a lone dancing man at a public park or outdoor concert. The man boogies to music, not caring that people are staring at him.

Soon, the dancing man's first follower arrives to dance with him. The first follower calls out to friends to join them, and then a few more people follow suit. Then a few more. Pretty soon, a crowd

---

1   https://www.ted.com/talks/derek_sivers_how_to_start_a_movement?language=en

of people is dancing to the music. Eventually, those who aren't dancing are the outliers.

So, who was the leader in this situation? The original dancing man, for sure. But the first follower, the man who dared to join the "disruptive" dancing dude, is the unsung leader. Without him, the crowd would not have followed. As an effective leader, you must have the courage to follow and show others how to follow.

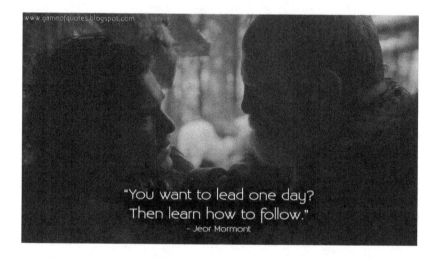

"You want to lead one day?
Then learn how to follow."
- Jeor Mormont

Do yourself a favor and seize opportunities to embrace your organization's disruptions, whether it's supporting new leadership or learning a new software system. Advocate the upside of these changes to your peers. Be brave. Force yourself to learn something new. Look for the benefits and share those benefits with your peers.

For example, technology has always scared me a little. Back in the olden days when I was a sales manager, I had zero interest in learning how to use the (gasp) world wide web. I fought against it tooth and nail. That is until I learned that I could shop on it. Holy cow!

After that, I preached the gospel of technology and the Internet to anyone who would listen! Show your organization that you are a leader by embracing disruptions. Be the first to dance with the dancing guy.

In conclusion

As I said, the red carpet to leadership is rarely rolled out in front of you. But, if you follow the steps that I have laid out for you, I know that you can accelerate your track to leadership.

Know your worth and don't be afraid to share these strengths with your bosses.

Be an advocate for yourself, and your employers and peers will follow.

Be a silo-buster. If you know that parts of your organization are unhealthy, don't get stuck in the muck! Take charge. Galvanize your peers and a trusted leader, and implement change from within.

And finally, be the first to embrace disruptions like new tech or leadership. All companies need to embrace change to stay innovative. Be a pioneer of that change, and you will prove to your peers and bosses that you are a leader.

FAIL. GROW. REPEAT.

*"Failure is a part of the process. You
just learn to pick yourself up."*

—Michelle Obama

I WISH YOU ALL a healthy, happy, and prosperous year filled with failures.

What? Yes, you read that right. Why is a book on leadership wishing you failure? Simple: failure can be the leading indicator of future success.

Fail. Grow. Repeat. This is a recipe for success. Henry Ford famously said, "Failure is simply the opportunity to begin again, this time more intelligently." I believe this to be true to my very core.

As a leadership consultant and executive coach, I wouldn't have a profession without failure— both my failures and the failures of the leaders I strive to develop. The more failure occurs, the more experience is gained, and the more lessons are learned on how to improve.

When I was a 27-year-old front-line sales manager, I truly believed that I had created the highest-performing culture in the history of sales organizations. My team was consistently ranked the number one team in the company.

To this day, my peers and team members from that time still talk about how they all drank the Kool-Aid.

Ahhh, the perspective that time and experience have given me. I take pride in the fact that my team over-achieved and out-performed. I pushed and empowered them, they delivered, and we all basked in our many rewards. We are all still connected to each other in some way or another today.

But just because we were successful doesn't mean that I was perfect. I know now that I was lucky to experience that level of success because boy oh boy was I failing at some key things.

My approach to leadership back then could be boiled down to a desire to be both loved and feared. I had yet to understand that "respected" was the best way to go. Let me count just a few of the ways that my idea of leadership showed up in harmful ways for my team:

1. Yelling. As the product of an Italian, Irish and Polish upbringing, I thought this was a completely normal way to communicate.

2. Horrible emails sent with bolded red words. I mean, if I yelled in person, my emails might as well yell too.

3. Need for unequivocal loyalty like a Mafia Godmother.

I got away with much of the above because I had built up the trust of my team. There was, however, an *AHA* moment for me. I call this moment my Mary Tyler Moore experience. Only I, unfortunately, was the female Lou Grant (and now I have revealed my age).

My team rarely challenged me over my yelling. This particular day, on a tough conference call, I knew I had gone too far but hoped my message was strong enough to overcome my delivery. It wasn't, and when the team rallied together to debrief with each other after the call, they selected the most unlikely spokesperson to confront me.

Julie was the kindest, least confrontational member of my team. That day, she came storming into my office and shut the door. Shaking like Mary Richards, she proceeded to raise her voice and tell me, "You can't talk to us like that." She was going to get her point across to me even though she was petrified.

In the moment, I tried not to show any outward reaction. I simply said, "You're right," and that was the end of that conversation. Her words and the courage it took to say them to me stayed with me, though. It still took me years to really get my yelling under control, but this experience allowed me to recognize and acknowledge that yelling was a failure. It was my first step towards growth.

As I have said, I was lucky. I did enough of the right things to secure a strong foundation. When "Hurricane Shelley" occasionally bore down, the house was left standing.

That said, keeping the same house standing isn't always what's needed for an organization to truly grow. I have worked with organizations where the leadership teams have stayed the same for over 20 years. Studies prove that change is essential for innovation,[2] and innovation makes for a thriving business.

When I walk into a company, I know that I will fail at some of my objectives to help make structural changes. Change is hard and scary! It fills us with uncertainty and fear of the unknown. More often than not, implementing change in an organization is an uphill battle filled with political landmines.

I have seen several of my clients struggle with this, especially as they try to grow an organization that has become stagnant. They are looking for my help and guidance but don't know how to pull out the first Jenga block— and if they do, they are afraid that the whole company structure will come crumbling down. Often, they know in their guts that what worked well for their once-thriving company is not working anymore.

2   https://www.forbes.com/sites/mikemyatt/2012/02/07/how-to-lead-change-3-simple-steps/#5c903ce2400b

I have played and coached sports the majority of my life, so I use a lot of sports analogies when I'm working with executives. The late great basketball coach Pat Summitt is one of the main people I find myself using as a mental North Star when I'm trying to keep things on track. She is a personal hero of mine who coached for 38 seasons at Tennessee with a 1,098-208 (.840) overall record while graduating 100 percent of her players. I quote her often, and her quote on loyalty is very applicable when I start trying to convince executives to make changes:

"The absolute heart of loyalty is to value those people who tell you the truth, not just those people who tell you what you want to hear. In fact, you should value them the most. Because they have paid you the compliment of leveling with you and assuming you can handle it."

If an organization has employees who care enough to initiate tough conversations and then stick around for them, they've already got the key ingredient for successful growth. It's just a matter of whether the executives can listen to the people who can tell them the WHOLE truth, not just the pretty bits.

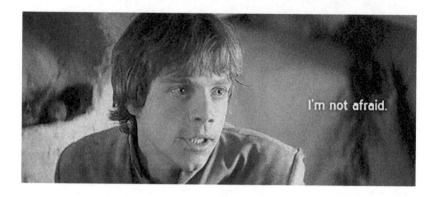

I tell struggling leaders that an effective coach must not get too engrossed in the game or they might miss a key substitution, a critical time-out, or the clock may run out before you know it. I tell them a good coach must metaphorically fly above the court to focus on the team as a whole. An effective leader must do the same.[3]

When I work with executives, I take that deep breath and tell them why they are failing. I tell them to float above their business and look at the whole court. When a leader can see all the failings happening on the court, then they make the best choices for the team as a whole.

Why are organizations not allowing for failure amongst their leadership teams? Why aren't they promoting failure? And why are leadership teams not doing the same for their front-line teams? We are so scared to fail, even when we know that one of the biggest reasons companies stagnate is an inability to accept failure as an acceptable option.

---

3   https://www.businessinsider.com/study-says-failure-can-help-you-suc-ceed-2015-5

So what has specifically gone wrong and how can they fix it? How will allowing failure lead to success?

I have found that allowing someone to stay in the same position for more than three years results in a lack of growth. Those people experience the same thing every day; the problems have become easy to solve, and complacency has set in.

It is similar to the basketball player who makes 90 percent of their free throws. This part of the game has become simple muscle memory, and they can do it blindfolded. But can that same player rebound? If not, can we put them in a position to learn? Can we allow them to fail before they succeed?

Yes, we can, and we should do so immediately. The result is fast growth and better performance. People often fall prey to thinking that just because they aren't naturally gifted at something means they will never be good at it. In reality, initial failure[4] doesn't generally act as a good predictor of later success. New talents can be cultivated if time and effort are invested in the process, and from there all that's left to do is to pick another skill and repeat!

A leadership team that has been in the same job for 20-plus years may have failed, grown, failed, and grown again in the early days of the organization, but slowly these failures became few and far between. The players have committed their performance to muscle memory.

If we reviewed their overall contributions, we would find that they turn in the same performance every year. They can maintain the status quo, or hit nominal growth targets within existing

---

4   https://www.theatlantic.com/education/archive/2018/04/the-value-of-failing/558848/

categories, but you cannot count on them for rapid growth and innovation.

We need to move folks around if we want that to change. They need to try different positions within the organization's ecosystem. They need to fail at new skills, grow from the lessons learned while failing, and repeat the process until more and more skills are perfected. This needs to be a strategy that leaders are willing to implement, and that aspiring leaders use to seek out growth opportunities. New positions = new failures. Failures = new growth.

People learn in many ways, but *experience*, is the best teacher.

We need to develop a corporate culture where it is safe to fail.[5] This is critically important to the new millennials moving into leadership roles. They will thrive in safe environments where their failures turn to success. The key is to coach them through the lessons learned so they can grow from them in real-time and move on to their next failures.

---

5   https://www.london.edu/faculty-and-research/lbsr/failure-the-key-to-success

I have witnessed the failures of many clients— both the kind that they grew from and the kind that ended up tanking the company. There was the EVP of Sales and Marketing at a huge organization that was making sales PowerPoint presentations because she couldn't empower her supervisees to do them for fear they wouldn't be as good as what she could do.

This was a clear failure to delegate which led to performance issues for everyone involved. The supervisees didn't feel like their boss trusted them to do their jobs, and the EVP's time was eaten up by building presentations instead of the higher-level tasks she could have been doing.

I played the Pat Summitt role and quickly and candidly told them that was crazy. We needed to work on the root cause of her control issues. Once we did, she changed and grew as a leader and started letting go for the greater good.

Unfortunately, not all leaders or aspiring leaders take the need to change and grow seriously. One time I worked with the founder of a software company who thought he could delegate to his team... but his idea of delegating was putting together lists that were pages long and contained every detail about every single task that needed to be done.

I never did get him to change, and I advised him to remove himself from his company if he wanted it to be successful. He didn't, the company failed, and the blame was laid at the feet of the poor team that was just trying to honor his every wish.

I could literally fill this book with examples. The bottom line is that we all fail in some way. The good news is that, through failure,[6] most of us learn and grow. Once we do, we need to keep repeating the process.

So fail on, leaders! Just make sure you are growing from the lessons learned and never getting complacent with where you stand.

---

6   https://www.success.com/why-failure-is-good-for-success/

<u>Author alert: proceed reading next chapter with caution.</u>

This chapter invokes a more strident tone than the other chapters in this book. While my goal throughout this book (including this chapter) is to educate my readers on leadership strategies that will help them become more effective, this chapter does that with a bit of attitude. Truth be told, this was the first chapter I wrote for this book. It was the very subject of the Gender Pay Gap that allowed me to turn my passion for pay equality into words that might help other females struggling with this. If the tone comes across too forceful for your reading pleasure, please skip to the next chapter. If you can accept the tone for the absolute passion it reflects, please continue reading on to learn how to negotiate and advocate for yourselves.

Negotiating the Gender Pay Gap: Why Hashtags Aren't Quite Enough

"I always thought that there was nothing an anti-feminist would want more than to have women only in women's organizations, in their own little corner empathizing with each other and not touching a man's world. If you're going to change things, you have to be with the people who hold the levers"

—Ruth Bader Ginsburg

THE GENDER WAGE gap has been on my mind for some time. In December 2017, I was scrolling through various news feeds trying to find a reprieve from negativity. I started browsing the entertainment posts and suddenly came face to face with some cold hard gender politics.

Award-winning actress Michelle Williams made approximately 0.7 percent of what her supporting co-star, Mark Wahlberg, made for reshoots of the Ridley Scott film *All the Money in the World* (the irony of the title doesn't pass me by). Williams was the star of the film—she carried the story. Yet she made $1,000 to his $1.5 million. That's a huge pay disparity.

The gender wage gap is not an isolated incident in the entertainment industry (or any industry). Claire Foy, who played Queen Elizabeth II in the television drama *The Crown* (and won a Golden Globe for her performance), made LESS than Matt Smith, who played her husband.

Once more for the people in the back: the woman playing the titular character and around whom the show revolves made less than the man playing second fiddle! Off with his head! Oh, wait, wrong queen.

My latest find yesterday was an article on the highest-paid television actors. Hurray for the male cast of *The Big Bang Theory*. All four male leads make between $23.5 million and $26 million per year for the show. It made me wonder what Mayim Bialik, one of the main female leads, is making on the same show. Forbes provided the answer: $12 million. Yes, almost 50 percent less. Blossom is getting screwed!

The stories of pay disparity in the entertainment world could easily be minimized as "Hollywood problems," but the sober reality is that the gender wage gap exists in every industry. Studies show that, on average, white women in the United States make approximately 80 cents for every dollar a white man makes.

Women of color make significantly less[7] than white women. Women are over-represented in low-wage jobs and under-represented in high-wage jobs. And globally, women earn 57 percent less than men.

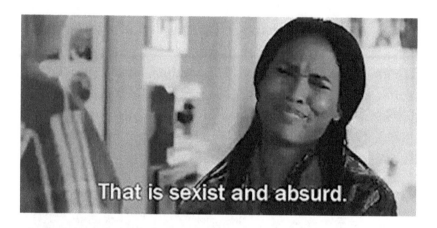

That is sexist and absurd.

All this inequality got me thinking about hashtags. I mean, who doesn't think about hashtags on the daily? But seriously, the past year we have seen how hashtags can bring about social awareness for important topics.

Actress Alyssa Milano shared her experience of sexual assault on Twitter, then encouraged people who had also been sexually assaulted to reply to her tweet with **#MeToo**, a movement founded by activist Tarana Burke in 2006. After Milano's tweet, a social phenomenon began with people all over the world speaking out about sexual assault and harassment.

#MeToo, #TimesUp, and **#BlackLivesMatter** have brought viral awareness of sexual assault, harassment in the workplace, and the violent and systemic racism against black people. The hashtag provides a tool to galvanize people all over the world

---

7   https://www.vox.com/identities/2018/4/10/17221282/equal-pay-day-women-of-color-disparity-gender-race-wage-gap

to verbalize injustices they dared not express before, including **#GenderPayGap.**

But now what? Hashtags have been vital to building awareness of critical issues, and awareness is the first step towards change, but where do we go from here? **#Whatsnext?**

It's not enough to use a trending hashtag; we need to translate those tweets into action. I've come up with just a few actions that we can start doing today to make a difference:

Educate ourselves! Learn why we have gender pay disparity, so we don't repeat the past.

1. Commit to speaking up and encourage others to do the same, even at the risk of upsetting the status quo.
2. Celebrate the companies that are committed to eradicating gender wage disparity and pass along the methods they used to get this done.
3. Arm ourselves with facts, so we know our value and can negotiate from a position of power.

Let's examine each of these strategies in more depth to see how to incorporate them into our daily lives.

Step One: Educate ourselves

To understand the gender pay gap, we need to understand the system that creates inequality. That system is patriarchy—a social construction in which men maintain power through the subordination of other men, women, and non-binary gender identities. In patriarchies, women are at a disadvantage socially, politically, and economically because they are not given the same privileges as men.

All of this patriarchy stuff began a long, long time ago. Historians have contrasting views about the birth of patriarchy, but it's been the prevalent mode of life for thousands of years. While there are examples of matriarchal societies,[8] in general men have historically maintained power through dominance and aggression against other men and women.

Examples of this are wars, burning women as witches, domestic violence, and slavery. For many hundreds of years, women were looked upon as commodities to be given away, traded, or sold for land, offspring, or wealth. It's the age-old, "I'll give you my virgin daughter for six camels and a plot of land" bit. Women have subsequently bought into patriarchal rule as a means of protection against men!

Along with their violent grab for power, men have historically maintained the status quo through an artificially created division of labor. Men were the breadwinners and women took care of the children and the home. This forced women to depend on men economically.

Another method of subduing women's power was not allowing them the same educational opportunities as men. Many women around the world continue to struggle for education equality.[9] By denying women an education and reducing their worth to that of a caregiver, we have systematically placed women at a disadvantage for centuries.

8   https://www.mydomaine.com/matriarchal-societies
9   https://www.brookings.edu/blog/brown-center-chalkboard/2018/04/23/
      how-our-education-system-undermines-gender-equity/

In the Forbes article about wage disparity called *"The Real Origins Of The Gender Pay Gap--And How We Can Turn It Around,"*[10] author Meghan Casserly describes presenting her mother with two imaginary candidates to hire for a teaching position: a man and a woman with equal qualifications. Her mother was in a pickle.

On the one hand, her mother worried that the man would not make enough to support his family, and on the other, she feared that the woman would take time off to get married and have kids.

Casserly writes, "... the subtle sexism at play in employment or salary decisions for men and women began to get clearer. A male employee is considered a breadwinner who should be valued—even above his pay grade—while a woman is at many turns a liability. As a result, across industries and education levels, it shows in their paychecks."

Casserly shares the compelling results of an annual survey that asks MBA candidates what they think they will earn at their first job out of school. Every female student reported that they

---

10   https://www.forbes.com/sites/meghancasserly/2012/07/05/real-origins-gender-pay-gap-how-we-can-turn-it-around/#1a30e3ad1e77

expected their first paycheck to be approximately $7,000 less than the male students. Casserly goes on to say that female students aren't just pulling these numbers out of thin air. The expected MBA annual salary for women is considerably less money a year than their male counterparts.

Men and women both contribute to the system of patriarchy. We can't help ourselves sometimes. Patriarchy has been normalized for thousands of years. We see the effects of this system in the job opportunities allotted to women and the generalized pay disparities across the board.

So, now that we have a better understanding of the roots of the gender pay disparity, what can we do? The next step is to speak up and get your family and friends on board.

Step Two: Speak up

Speak up about wage inequality and get your co-workers to do the same. Be a team! Is it such a radical idea that we have each other's backs on getting equal pay?

Once upon a time in a magical land called Hollywood, the cast of a hit television show called *Friends* banded together for equal pay. During the second season, David Schwimmer and Jennifer Aniston were making more money than the rest of the cast.

When salary negotiations began for the third season, Schwimmer and Aniston agreed to a salary cut so that everyone in the cast would get equal pay. If producers didn't agree to equal pay for every cast member moving forward, they would all quit. As a result, by the end of the show's run, they were all making a whopping 1 million dollars per episode.

Now those are some hard-core, supportive, team players! Co-workers in all labor industries must learn to support one another and sometimes make sacrifices in our fight for equal pay.

Step Three: Learn from success stories

If we study who is doing it right, we can discover a working model that all companies can use to fix wage disparity. In my quest to find a blueprint, I did a little research on the companies that have women's backs.

Starbucks – Good ol' Starbucks has achieved 100% equal pay across race and gender. How did they do this? For the past ten years, they have focused on equalizing compensation. And just as important, they focused on the behaviors and systemic problems that create the wage gap, like educational opportunities, supporting women who need pregnancy leave, retirement and investment plans, and tuition reimbursement.

Salesforce – In 2016, Salesforce, a cloud computing company, was one of more than 100 companies to sign Obama's Equal Pay Pledge and agree to conduct gender pay analyses every year to close the gap and eradicate bias in hiring and promotions.

One of the ways that Salesforce works on closing the gap is by making "equality" one of their core values. And core values start at the top. The CEO, Marc Benioff, calls for all CEOs to step up and take action against the gender wage gap. The company understands that closing the gap takes constant study and work. Salesforce spends millions every year conducting assessments of how their employees are paid, finding pay disparities, and fixing the problem.

Adobe – Computer software company Adobe also took the Equal Pay Pledge and said it has eradicated the gender wage gap. The company has made gender equality a long-term commitment, not only because it's the right thing to do, but also because it's good business.

Adobe's blog cites a study that shows companies with the greatest number of women are more likely to introduce radical innovations into the market. For a technology company like Adobe, innovation is the key to success.

Adobe is not only focused on closing the gender wage gap, but also fixing the system that creates the gap. Adobe does this by committing to the next generation of female employees. Adobe has given $3.5 million to youth tech programs, including Girls Who Code. They also started the Abode Digital Academy, which teaches people in lower-opportunity job fields (which means lots of women and people of color) the skills they need to move into the tech world.

The company has also committed to hiring a diverse workforce by improving hiring practices and training HR managers to break through unconscious sexist and racist bias.

What did all these rock star companies do first and foremost to make a change? What is the blueprint that other companies can follow to eradicate the gender wage gap?

First, they became aware of their ingrained (and often subconscious) bias against women. Once they'd done some self-reflection and analysis, they consciously decided to make equality a core part of their culture. They continuously put time and money into finding problem areas and fixing them. All of these companies understand that closing the gap will take constant hard work and upkeep.

Step Four: Know our value

We need to arm ourselves with facts about salaries so we can negotiate our value from a position of power. How can we do this?

1. **Know your worth.** Remember this from the earlier chapter on accelerating your leadership? Well, it bears repeating here: figure out what unique qualities you bring to your company that enhances the performance of the organization. Write them down. Talk to your mentor(s) about them. Run them past your co-workers. Gain agreement about them from your boss.

2. **Look it up.** Research wages and salary using crowd-sourced information websites like Glassdoor, Indeed, Payscale, Salaryexpert, Salarylist, Fairygodboss.

3. **Print out** market and pay data information as proof in case someone wants to low-ball you.

4. Ask your male co-workers to help you. If they tell you their salaries, you will be armed with the most critical piece of information. If that fails, ask your HR team if they see a gender pay gap at your organization.

5. Learn how to successfully negotiate and then practice those skills! Find a buddy who can role-play the salary negotiation so that you can get comfortable talking about why you deserve a raise and can answer any questions or rebuttals your supervisor may have.

To sum everything up, the gender pay gap is a reality in the lives of almost all women, and it's something that we CAN stop. It will take a lot of hard work as individuals and as a team, but it's definitely possible—we have the case studies to prove it!

To think, all of this disparity talk started with me thinking about hashtags. During the past few years, many of us have become more aware of the gender wage gap because social injustices have been thrust into the public eye through these funny little catch phrases preceded by a pound sign.

Hashtags got me thinking about not only bringing awareness to pay disparity but to how we can fix it. We've seen it done with companies like Starbucks and Adobe, so we know it can be done.

We can fix this problem by educating ourselves about the history of patriarchy. We can speak out about the pay gap and encourage our co-workers to do the same. We can encourage businesses to emulate companies that are fighting to end wage disparity. And finally, we can get the facts about what we are worth as employees and negotiate pay based on our qualifications, not our gender.

History reflects the great strides that women have made in the workplace. But history also shows that we are still far from equality. Let's put our big girl britches on and work toward ending the gender wage gap once and for all.

3 "C-crets" for Building Thriving Teams in 2019

"Teamwork is the ability to work together toward a common vision. The ability to direct individual accomplishments toward organizational objectives. It is the fuel that allows common people to attain uncommon results."

–Andrew Carnegie

I ATTRIBUTE A LOT of my success in building strong teams to my passion for sports, especially basketball. For more than 30 years, I have played and coached basketball, a team sport that requires a group of skilled athletes, each with a unique role to play, to work toward a shared goal: winning.

My career as a sales leader turned leadership coach has been successful because I know the secret to triumphant teamwork. More days than not, I find myself imparting the same lessons learned on the court to my corporate clients:

"Practice until it becomes muscle memory and you can do it blindfolded."

"Communicate with each other."

"Move the ball around until you find the open man."

"Know where your teammates are at all times."

"How much time is left on the clock?"

These are just a few of the lessons that transfer from the basketball court to the conference room. Thriving teams — both on and off the court — share the same DNA. A successful team needs to:

- **Understand the purpose.** What's your goal? Win the game? Make a lot of money? Change the world?

- **Have confidence in the vision.** Is everyone on board with the mission statement?

- **Collaborate with and trust in each other.** The lone wolf dies, but the pack survives (thank you *Game of Thrones* for that one).

- **Rally around your teammates' successes.** Remember the old saying, "A rising tide lifts all boats."

- **Seek continuous growth and improvement** for the business and the team. Businesses die without innovation.

- **Recruit high-potential players.** I'll take LeBron James, thank you very much.

I could go on and on with a bullet point list of "50 Things You Can Do Right Now to Build a Better Team." Believe me, I've fallen asleep to those listicles and know how enticing they can be!

Instead, I've narrowed the requirements for building a high-performance team culture into THREE must-haves. I like to call them the 3 C's. The "C-cret" is that you need all 3 C's to thrive as a team. They are (drum roll please):

Communication

Clarity

and

Concern

As a leader, understanding and implementing the 3 C's can be the difference between a cohesive and productive team and complete chaos, and any aspiring leader needs to work to strengthen and practice these skills.

Thriving teams = High Performance. Chaos = Poor Performance. There's a fabulous diagram that I hang in my office as a constant reminder of the three things I need to be doing every single day.

I've included it on the following page for you, but it shows that the 3 C's make up the 3 points of a triangle with high-performing teams in the middle. If even one of those points is missing, the whole triangle collapses. Take a look, and if the visualization is helpful, I highly recommend printing it off and tacking it up somewhere you'll see it often!

Thriving Team:
The 3 "C-crets" to Developing a High-Performance Culture

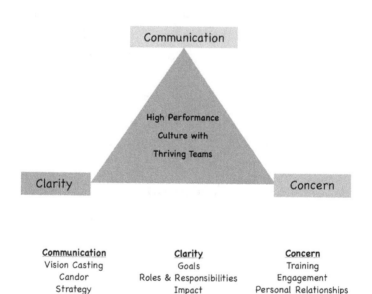

Communication	Clarity	Concern
Vision Casting	Goals	Training
Candor	Roles & Responsibilities	Engagement
Strategy	Impact	Personal Relationships
Results	Data	Performance Reviews
Recognition	Purpose	Trust

Without excelling at all 3 C's, you will never be able to create and sustain a team that maximizes performance. That brings us to another critical area of successful leadership: balance.

It might seem like common sense, but striving to be a well-rounded leader is one of the most significant steps you can take to building a thriving team. That's not to say that you have to be an expert at everything— you have your team for that!

However, you DO need to take the initiative to continually strengthen your skills and understanding in all of the areas that impact your work and your team.

Take a minute to do a self-assessment. If you had to rank your top three skills as a leader, what would they be? Communication? Implementing new technology? Supervising or managing others? Networking and building external relationships? Securing sustainable and flexible funding?

Once you've got a good grasp on what your strengths are, think about the areas where you feel like you're in over your head. Maybe you don't feel confident learning and utilizing the latest technology, or you're an introvert and making small talk in a room full of new investors sounds like torture. Perhaps you're great at communicating verbally, but your writing skills aren't quite as eloquent as you'd like. Does the thought of what your finance team members do make your head spin?

If you want to apply the 3 C-crets of **Communication, Clarity,** and **Concern** with maximum efficacy, you need to have a solid grasp of what your strengths and weaknesses are as a leader (or leader-to-be). Once you know where you stand, you can take action to address any barriers to implementing the 3 C's!

For example, say you don't feel confident in your understanding of new technology that might benefit your projects. In order to have true clarity about the appropriate roles and responsibilities of each team member, you need to minimally know what implementing the new technology requires in terms of experience, skill set, and attitude. If you don't know that, you won't be able to select the best people for the job!

Once you've got clarity, that naturally flows into a better ability to communicate your vision for how the new technology might benefit your team and broader organization.

As a bonus, if you know enough to select the team members who are best-suited to the task, you'll be showing concern for your team. Nobody likes their skills being overlooked or being forced onto a project that doesn't align with their talents. So, if you're able to pick the right people, it makes them feel validated and prevents frustration for everyone.

You could apply the same thinking to just about any sample scenario your team might face. However, being able to pull all of that off hinges on you knowing your strengths and weaknesses and taking the initiative to fill in any big gaps! For areas of weakness, a quick Google search can often unearth a trove of information. If that's not cutting it, then figure out who on your team or in your organization has the information you need and can help you learn.

It might seem counterproductive to admit to team members that you don't fully understand something when you're trying to play the part of a fearless leader. As Brene Brown[11] would say, though, "Imperfections are not inadequacies; they are reminders that we're all in this together."

Team members don't need a leader who knows everything all of the time. They need someone who is self-aware and isn't afraid to keep it real about what their strengths and limitations are.[12] Being authentic about who you are and what you bring to the

---

11   https://www.ted.com/talks/brene_brown_on_vulnerability
12   https://www.forbes.com/sites/kevinkruse/2013/05/12/what-is-authentic-leadership/#72bbab34def7

table sends a powerful message to your team: you have skills, but you also recognize that they have their own expertise, and at the end of the day you're all in this together.

The ripple effect of setting up an environment where team members can play to their strengths and shine is massive. It cultivates new leaders within your team and shows that you trust them to do what they need to do to succeed.

When team members feel like you've got their backs and are actively seeking the best path forward for the entire team — and not just yourself — engagement skyrockets.

You have the ability to set the tone for your team, and they'll follow your lead. If you're closed off and don't communicate or show concern, they'll reflect that same attitude to you. But if you implement the 3 C-crets and incorporate communication, clarity, and concern into your daily interactions, you'll be well on your way to a high-performing team!

If you're wondering exactly how to make sure that you're using the 3 Cs effectively, you're in luck— in the next couple of chapters I'll take a deep dive into each of them and what they mean for your leadership.

In my discussion of the 3Cs, I describe them in action from the perspective of a leader at the top of an organization, showing how they impact overall functioning. Don't mistake this, though, for the same three tools are essential for leaders at any level. You must nurture and hone them if you want to enhance your ability to reach your leadership goals.

So as you read, try to visualize how the 3Cs in action at the very top of an organization apply to you and your team elsewhere. And print off that triangle, hang it on your wall, and let's get down to business!

C-Cret #1: COMMUNICATION

*"Communication is a skill that you can learn.
It's like riding a bicycle or typing. If you're
willing to work at it, you can rapidly improve
the quality of every part of your life."*

– Brian Tracy

As a leader, what and how you communicate sets the overall tone for your company's culture — or your team. You are the head coach and general manager of your organization. As such, you need to focus on what and how you **communicate** the following to your team:

Vision

You are responsible for communicating the organization's vision. If I'm the coach of the Celtics, my vision is winning the NBA Championship. Every player on my team must share the same goal. If someone on the team doesn't share the vision, they're not a team player. My assistants all share and communicate the same vision in their work.

The same needs to be true for your organization. Communicate your vision early and often. Get everyone on board.[13] Ask your employees to articulate your shared vision during meetings.

---

13   https://www.entrepreneur.com/article/285500

Heck, ask them when you pass them in the halls. It can be helpful to revisit your vision during performance reviews to see what your employee's understanding of the vision is and how they see themselves fitting into it.

Strategy

How is your team going to meet the organization's vision? Think, "We are going to win the NBA championship and here's how..." Every great coach has a playbook. Share these plays with your team so everyone knows the strategy to win the game, to make the profit, or to find the genius new hires.

Please do not make the mistake of only having this conversation with your direct reports. As the leader, you must set the tone.[14] The entire team needs to hear the strategy from you, not just your assistant coaches.

Don't attempt to develop your strategy in isolation! Your role is to synthesize all of the moving pieces in the organization and figure out how to keep them all headed in the same direction, but that doesn't mean you have to go it alone.

---

14   https://www.forbes.com/sites/mikemyatt/2012/04/04/10-communica-
tion-secrets-of-great-leaders/#6d7671dd22fe

Think of the old saying, "Two heads are better than one." Many of the most influential leaders have a close group of people they bounce ideas off of and get feedback from. Figure out who should be on your war council — team members with specific expertise, key players in the organization, industry experts, and newcomers with fresh perspective are just a few of the people you might want to include.

It will be a lot easier to confidently communicate your strategy when you know that it's already been picked apart and put back together by multiple people. That confidence can make or break whether your team sees the strategy as a win or as a train wreck waiting to happen.

Candor

How you communicate your organization's performance, challenges, and successes will determine how your team rallies around you as a leader. Simply put, be candid with them. There is an endless supply of research that shows a direct correlation between a lack of honesty and poor performance.

According to Conflict Dynamics Profile,[15] a lack of transparency creates mistrust and fear, stifles innovation, allows poor performance to be overlooked, and normalizes "group think." Do not allow room for water-cooler speculation. An informed team, whether the news is good or bad, is a team that will rally, be more productive, and trust in the company's vision.

As a side note, being candid does not mean being a jerk. A culture of transparency is not about pointing out people's faults in a mean way. Helpful candid conversations should be about, "... helping, mentoring, and being a good colleague."

That is the ugliest effing skirt I have ever seen.

---

15   https://www.conflictdynamics.org/

Results

Don't limit your communications about your business results to once a quarter — or even worse, once a year. If everyone on your team is living in the dark about the organization's failures and successes, then nobody knows if they need to make changes or not.

Give your direct reports feedback on their results as often as possible. Hold monthly "town hall" meetings with your entire organization and communicate this information. A well-informed team is a strong team. Nobody can make positive changes if they don't know what's going on.

Recognition

Celebrate your individual and team wins early and often. Small wins, big wins, great ideas that led to wins — we all need a pat on the back at times. When you recognize your teammate's successes, they feel valued. Studies show that when employees feel valued, productivity and motivation will improve.

Also, make sure that your assistant coaches are following your lead. Celebrate their wins, but make sure they are celebrating their own team's successes as well.

Dialogue vs. Debate vs. Demand

When you communicate with your team, there are three main approaches: dialogue, debate, and demand. They each serve different purposes[16] and will result in different outcomes, so knowing when to use each approach is crucial.

- **Dialogue** is generally a good default approach because it is non-combative and seeks to increase understanding for all parties involved. When you open up a dialogue with your team, you're sharing information about what you want to do and providing space for team members to offer their perspectives.

  Dialogue is particularly beneficial when you're making large decisions about the vision, strategy, and direction of the team. It allows team members to feel like they have a stake in the outcome, and it provides you with an opportunity to hear about the topic from perspectives you might not have considered.

  The goal of dialogue is not to change anyone's mind. Instead, you're merely trying to discuss things and understand everyone's point of view. For example, if your team encountered an unexpected barrier, you might use dialogue to introduce your plan and hear from your team members about whether they think the plan will work and any other considerations.

- **Debate** is typically only productive if you're looking to pick apart an idea or strategy and don't necessarily need everyone to leave feeling heard and invested. A debate is

---

16   https://www.ccl.org/articles/leading-effectively-articles/communication-1-idea-3-facts-5-tips/

far more oppositional than dialogue; there are two or more sides to the conversation, with each side trying to convince the other(s) why they are wrong.

Debate can be incredibly useful if you have a team of self-assured individuals who enjoy getting into the weeds of an issue. It will provide you with an opportunity to hear the most compelling arguments for and against a given plan of action, which can provide you with vital insight on how to move forward.

The downside is that, for team members who don't feel strongly about the issue or who are non-confrontational, a debate can cause disengagement. Use debate strategically, and pay attention to your team dynamics to make sure that people aren't checking out or leaving the table feeling too discouraged.

- **Demand** is going to be used sparingly by most good leaders. If you're demanding something, there is no room for dialogue or debate — what you say is the end-all-be-all.

You might need to use demand if you're having conversations about accountability, e.g., "You need to increase your performance in this way, or you will be terminated." When used appropriately, demand can result in substantial action without eroding the relationship between you and your team.

If used indiscriminately, however, demand can quickly sour the relationship between you and your team and give you a reputation for being a dictator.

At the end of the day, as long as you are communicating intentionally, you can fine-tune things as you go. Being aware of the different aspects to communication is the biggest hurdle, and if you can consistently keep in mind how you're communicating the vision, strategy, and results in a way that is candid and celebratory you'll be on the right track!

C-cret #2: CLARITY

*Clarity (noun): clearness or lucidity as
to perception or understanding; freedom
from indistinctness or ambiguity*

CLARITY IS THE next must-have C in our triangle. Once you have communicated the vision and strategy, your team needs clarity around how they will contribute to the success of the organization.

I have had many clients struggle with clarity. They have employees that don't know how they fit into the team, and as a result, struggle aimlessly to have any impact. Your players need to understand their role to thrive.

This clarity needs to start at the top. Something as simple as a job description is often missing from poorly performing organizations. You cannot expect your teams to thrive without clarity. Make sure your teams and players are clear about the following:

Goals

As a leader, you need to be crystal clear with every single employee about both team and individual goals. Have an employee handbook that everyone gets with your organization's mission clearly stated, as well as each employee's unique mission depending on their job.

For example, the goal of the basketball team is to win the game. The goal of the shooting guard is to score points and steal the ball. If you can't articulate the specific goals of each person on your team and how that connects to the organizational mission, now's the time to figure that out!

Also, be sure to revisit whatever handbooks and job descriptions you have on a regular basis. Having a job description doesn't do you any good if nobody has looked at it since it was created five years ago!

Attaining clarity regarding organizational and individual goals is an ongoing process. Think about how you can set aside time on an annual or semi-annual basis to do a sweep of all the documents, job descriptions, and handbooks you use to make sure they're still in line with your goals.

If you struggle to pare everything you want to achieve down to a few measurable goals, try coming up with separate goals for set periods of time. Have 6-month goals, one-year goals, 3-year goals, 5-year goals, and 10-year goals.

Having things broken out in this way will make it easier for you to clearly communicate — both verbally and in writing — how each person on your team fits into accomplishing those goals.

Roles and responsibilities

Make sure that every single job in your organization has clearly defined roles and responsibilities that are presented in writing every year. Again, this will go in your employee handbook.

Knowing your role and responsibilities is vital because it sets clear boundaries and goals for the individual. I've known people who worked in management that seemed to wear too many hats. They worked over 70 hours a week doing everything because their leaders never gave them a set list of responsibilities and a clear definition of their role.

They burned out and ultimately couldn't do their best work because they were a frazzled shell of a human being. If everyone knows their roles and responsibilities, everything gets done with less energy wasted.

When you're doing your annual review of the roles and responsibilities, use that opportunity to have a conversation with your team members about what adjustments or tweaks might make sense. Maybe AJ has always been a front-lines trainer but has recently discovered a talent for logistical coordination.

It might make sense to adjust the roles and responsibilities to capitalize on individual talents, rather than choose to a) keep them in the same role as before, or b) technically keep them in the same role as before, but expect them to take on new responsibilities anyway.

Impact

Simply put, everyone should clearly understand the impact their role has on the organization and its goals. If your copy editor doesn't care that there's a typo on the website, then they do not understand their role in the organization, and your organization suffers because it looks unprofessional.

Another example is if an employee doesn't know that their weekly business newsletters are helping morale. Without that insight, they don't know what a great impact they are having on the team and might lose motivation or think it won't matter if they stop doing the newsletters.

Figure out how each of your team members likes to receive validation for their work. For some people, it might drive home the impact they have on the team if you recognize them publicly for their contributions at a staff meeting or banquet.

Other employees might want to crawl under the table if you put the spotlight on them and would much prefer a short card, email, or one-on-one conversation.

Regardless of what they prefer, the important thing is that you find a way to do it. When team members understand and can see or hear the direct impact that they have on an organization and clientele, they are much more likely to remain invested in their job and see what they do as meaningful.

Data

As leaders, it's our job to understand the data and clearly articulate the meaning of that data to our teams. Break it down so that it is easily understood; don't just data-dump a report in an email. Hold a meeting where you can share the information with the entire team. Make it brief and easy to understand.

Also, make sure it's accurate! I went to a board meeting once where the director of operations passed out a spreadsheet of the year's debts and earnings, and none of the numbers added up. That was embarrassing and brought morale down for the whole team.

Data doesn't just mean numbers, either. For many businesses, there are plenty of metrics and numbers you can pull regarding sales, client satisfaction, staff performance, and more.

For social service organizations, though, data often seems less relevant. Keep in mind that data also means stories from clients and people that your organization interacts with! Try to identify how you can capture those stories and anecdotal evidence that you can present to your team — and funders, board members, and the community at large.

The more concrete points of reference you can give your team, the more likely they are to have clarity on how things are going and what might need to change.

Purpose

What is the objective of my organization? Why does my role exist? What is the justification behind a, b, and c? These are questions that should be answered as often as necessary so that your team thoroughly understands their purpose, both individually and as a thriving team.

If your team doesn't understand why they need to win the championship, innovate new technology, or hire a new copy editor because the last one left typos on the business website, then nothing will get done!

Think of your purpose as a sort of North Star for you and your organization. It's what you can use to navigate toward your destination, whatever that might be. Without clarity about your purpose, you'll just be drifting along at the mercy of the currents.

However, if you and your team all share the same North Star and understand how your individual roles can help move the organization in that direction, you'll be able to expertly navigate anything thrown your way!

C-Cret #3: CONCERN

"Dispirited, unmotivated, unappreciated workers cannot compete in a highly competitive world."

—Francis Hesselbein

Perhaps the most overlooked of the three Cs is **Concern**. As a leader, coach, or manager, our teams need to trust that we do what we do because we are concerned about their success. We should always be striving to show that concern in the following ways:

Training and Development

I am always surprised when I take on a struggling new client, and they don't have a consistent or scalable training and development strategy. Even worse is when the company got rid of its training and development department in a bid to cut costs. Yikes!

By the time I'm in the room, the client has identified the need for a coach to help them achieve peak performance. What they fail to do is to make the connection that all of their employees need coaching too. When individuals face challenges at work, if they can identify the challenge but don't know how to solve the problem, then their employers are failing them.

I've seen intelligent and hardworking employees fail at their jobs because nobody taught them what to do. Show your teams that you are concerned about their success and put training and development into your budget and strategy.

Be sure to talk to your teams about what training or professional development would be meaningful for them before you sign them up for anything! There might be opportunities that are on their radar that you have no idea about; don't be afraid to go outside the box when it comes to training and development.

Going to a conference on racial justice and equity might not seem relevant to a sales position on the surface, but there are innumerable ways that an employee might use that experience to improve your organization and strengthen their sales strategies!

Engagement

As leaders, we need raving fans, and raving fans evolve from engaged employees. What is employee engagement? Well, according to Forbes writer Kevin Kruse,[17] "Employee engagement is the emotional commitment the employee has to the organization and its goals."

That means that employees care about their work and the goals of the organization. Sure, they like the paycheck and vacation days, but overall, they love their job. They are fans!

Engaged employees are more likely to work harder, go above and beyond, and act in the best interest of their company. Kruse said, "Engaged employees lead to better business outcomes."

17   https://www.forbes.com/sites/kevinkruse/2012/06/22/employee-engage-ment-what-and-why/#4313ff067f37

So, how does a business engage its employees? There are count-less ways! Make sure your employees understand their goals and responsibilities. Not understanding what their goals and responsibilities are will make people anxious and unhappy in the workplace. Remember everything in the chapter on clarity, and you'll be off to a good start on creating engaged employees.

It's not that I'm lazy, it's that I just don't care.

Show concern for any issue that might arise and make an effort to help fix it. Or better yet, get your employees the training they need so they feel happy and confident fixing the problem them-selves. When you're planning out the direction you want your organization to go, set a goal to establish an employee engage-ment program.

Personal relationships

You can't and shouldn't endeavor to be best friends with your employees. You can, however, show concern about non-work aspects of their lives. Share a little about yourself as well!

This is an easy thing to work into your existing supervision practices. I like to start team meetings by asking everyone to briefly share one personal success story and one business success story that they have achieved since the last meeting. If we all consistently show that we care about each other's lives, we bond as a team. Bonding builds better collaboration, communication, and teamwork.

When you create space for employees to bring their whole selves into the work, you'll have far better luck cultivating strong relationships. It goes a long way for your team to know that you see them as more than just the work they produce — you recognize that they are human beings with lives outside of the office.

I've sometimes heard from concerned managers that, if they let personal lives into the office, it will cause drama and employees will lose respect for them. News flash: if your employees stop respecting you because you admitted that there's more to them than their job, they never respected you in the first place.

Obviously, there is always a chance that drama can happen— but then, that chance exists no matter what you do as a supervisor. In the vast majority of organizations I've worked with, when managers are understanding and invested in supporting their employees holistically, the employees actually try even harder not to let personal stuff get in the way at work.

There's a mutual respect; the supervisor respects that the job isn't the end-all-be-all, and the employee respects that the supervisor still needs work to get done (and done well).

Performance reviews

Consistent and comprehensive performance reviews are the number one way to show concern for your employees' success. In a performance review, you can mutually discuss their strengths and weaknesses.

Tell them all the ways you see them positively contributing to the company. It never hurts to build someone's esteem. A happy and confident employee will only work better and harder.

Talk about the weaknesses, but don't just cut them down — have a dialogue about what their options are for improvement.[18] If someone has been struggling with the technological side of the job, be proactive and get them some training. They will appreciate the help; after all, you're helping them better themselves in a way that might help them move up in the company.

---

18   https://www.15five.com/blog/9-ways-to-give-effective-employee-feedback/

Allow them space to discuss where they see themselves in the company and have a discussion about it. Get on the same page. Do they want to move up? Create a plan for advancement together.

Performance reviews are one of your best opportunities to have frank conversations with your team and to check in with them about what's working and what's not. No matter how busy your schedule gets, prioritize carving out time to make performance reviews happen.

If they fall by the wayside, you might end up unintentionally sending the message to your employees that you've got more important things to do than spend that short amount of time with them.

Also, you don't have to wait for a performance review if there is something pressing to address. Ideally, you have regular one-on-ones or check-ins with each team member and can address performance issues as they arise. You don't want to save up every minor infraction from the past six months and dump it on them at their performance review!

Instead, address things as they happen and use the performance review as a time to highlight overall trends in their performance, celebrate successes, and plan for the future.

I don't trust you!

Trust

Trust your team to do their jobs. The micro-manager never wins (and usually burns out and is hated by everyone). Show your employees that you trust them by delegating responsibilities. Give them the space to ask for help if they need it, but don't offer unsolicited advice.

By giving your team this chance to prove themselves capable of the job, they are building confidence in themselves, and you are building trust in your employees. Thriving teams consistently outperform their competition because they have learned confidence through trust.

If you're able to incorporate all 3 Cs — communication, clarity, and concern — into your supervision and leadership, you'll find yourself on the fast track to a high-performing team. Remind yourself to be clear about roles and responsibilities and to have concern for your employees who might need training or increased engagement.

The key is to have a way to hold yourself accountable and stay on track with incorporating the 3 Cs into your leadership. Whether that's another member of your leadership team, a mentor, or your director — make sure you've got a system in place to hold yourself accountable. If you can do that, you'll see the results in no time!

THE 5 MINUTE MINDSET AND SKILL SET ASSESSMENT

"If my future were determined just by my performance on a standardized test, I wouldn't be here. I guarantee you that."

—Michelle Obama

I CAN'T STRESS ENOUGH how important it is to your success as a leader for you to continuously assess yourself and your employees.

Why?

Regular assessments can become your #1 communication tool. When employees know where they stand, employee engagement increases. Leading people means communicating their performance goals as well as communicating the measurement of those goals.

Leading also means communicating performance throughout the organization so that training and development can be tailored to employee needs. Effective leadership and communication also ensure that proper recognition and reward opportunities are developed.

The first thing I do when I engage with a new client is to ask for unimpeded access to assess their teams. It is critical to understand where they are so that I can develop a success plan that takes what I call their "Mindsets" and "Skill Sets" into account.

In some organizations, I have hundreds of people to assess, so I created a simple tool that allows me to conduct an assessment in five minutes. This tool became so useful for me that I taught many of my clients how to use it themselves to continuously assess not only their supervisees, but their peers as well. We will walk through exactly how this powerful tool works later in this chapter.

The one element that never changes regardless of organization size, success, products, or service sold is that there is always, always room for growth. However, you cannot grow as an organization if you don't have a starting point, and assessments provide you with that.

There are many different companies out there that provide assessments that evaluate candidates during the hiring process. I have used several, and I do believe in their value. It's never too early to begin the assessment process so that you have a solid baseline understanding of where all potential employees are.

Annual reviews exist in most successful organizations. When I was a sales leader, I dreaded the administrative nightmare that accompanied the review season. At one point in my career, I had 27 direct reports, and completing and delivering the 10-page corporate review process in the two weeks that were allocated was a living hell.

My peers and I would scream, "This is the wrong time to do this — it's the end of the year!" and "We don't even have time to eat and sleep — is HR crazy?" For me, review season meant 270 pages and 27 hours of review with each of my direct reports. Suffice it to say; it was one of the most challenging administrative tasks that we endured.

I use the word task because that is how we all looked at the process: one nightmarish task. The problem was, the nightmare was self-created.

I have always been an ardent proponent of regular one-on-one meetings with my team members. My training background has taught me the art and value of delivering balanced feedback early and often so that people always know their strengths and weaknesses and can plan their development accordingly.

The coach in me is always ready to provide immediate feedback and ideas on course correction:

"Don't stop your dribble until you know what you want to do with the ball!"

"Find the open space!"

"Stop heaving up bricks!"

I brought this coaching approach to the corporate environment with ease. I used to create my own annual review nightmare because I never took the time to write things down or look at the situation holistically. I was coaching tasks and occasionally impacting attitude or mindset, but I wasn't taking the time to understand how assessments connected throughout the organization.

Vowing to never go through that administrative hell, I took apart the 10-page review form and focused on 3-4 things I wanted to review with each of my reports on a quarterly basis. The experience was dramatically improved for everyone involved. I still never thought it was ideal, but we all benefited far more from the new model.

Here are some of the reasons why adjusting the approach to assessment changed the impact it had:

- **We communicated,** particularly about job responsibilities, goals, and obstacles. It was an opportunity to be open and candid with each other. As a supervisor, it was informative for me to see both what was spoken during these meetings and what was unspoken. For example, an employee that offered no self-assessment or had no questions to ask presented a red flag.

- **Employee engagement increased.** Reducing turnover is a common goal in most successful organizations. One of the best ways to accomplish that is to foster employee engagement.

  I personally become "all in" when I know what my goals are and what the expectations are for my performance. The same was true for all of my employees. When they were clear on their goals, knew where to go for help with their obstacles, and knew exactly what they had to do to be successful, their level of engagement was consistently high.

- **Clear and realistic development plans were established.** We openly discussed development opportunities and what steps could be taken for self-development.

  No basketball player steps on the court and shoots 100 percent. It is understood that success takes many hours of practice, and a good deal of that practice needs to be self-directed. It is, however, our responsibility as leaders to give our employees "practice plans."

- **Career Pathing.** The assessment process also provides the opportunity to discuss career next steps and put appropriate pathing plans in place.

- **Take action on poor performers.** Note I said, "take action." The number one mistake leaders make that impacts their teams is to allow poor performance to continue without consequence or action. This is an absolute culture crusher, as consistent performers feel their achievements don't matter when underachievers are given a pass. You must take action!

Put employees who aren't meeting expectations on performance improvement plans. If they don't improve, fire or repurpose them. Do this in less than 90 days and you will earn and keep the respect of your top performers — and those are the people who matter most to the long-term success of your team.

It can help to put your disciplinary process in writing and include it in the employee handbook. Having it available to everyone takes some of the mystery out of it and makes sure that your approach is clear and consistent for all employees.

Both annual and quarterly reviews are a must for all of the reasons I mentioned above. The real truth, however, is you need to be assessing your team all of the time. So how do you do that? There are only so many hours in the day, and it is a real grind to do it yourself. The value is obvious, but it just isn't realistic.

The 5 Minute Mindset/Skill Set Evaluation was created to tackle this dilemma. This simple evaluation will provide you with all the information you need, you won't have to complete it on your own in a vacuum, and you will grow exponentially as a leader by implementing it.

This evaluation focuses on two key performance indicators: Mindset and Skill Set.

Mindset, as defined by Merriam-Webster, is a mental attitude or inclination. Simply put, "You are what you believe."

Keying in on and evaluating mindsets is a powerful tool.

Belief → Effort → Achievement

If people believe they can do something, they generally understand that effort will be required to be successful.

Leaders have to understand that they need to believe in order for their team to believe, put in the effort, and ultimately achieve.

The other part of the equation is the skill set. You must have the required skill set for achievement to be possible. It can be a skill set that is still being developed, but it must be present for success to follow.

I developed two 5 Minute Mindset/Skill Set evaluations. One is for leaders, and one is for individuals, but there are only minor differences. I looked at the premise that **belief → effort →achievement** and focused on how that can be demonstrated by leaders and performers. I then came up with the key measurement components for each. The following pages show what each assessment looks like:

MINDSET ASSESSMENT FOR LEADERSHIP

	Yes	No	Unsure
Share the Vision			
Focus on Growth			
Support the Overall Health of the Organization			
Promote Clarity and Transparency			

SKILL SET ASSESSMENT FOR LEADERSHIP

	Yes	No	Unsure
Produce Results			
Communicate Effectively			
Take Action			

MINDSET ASSESSMENT FOR INDIVIDUAL PERFORMERS

	Yes	No	Unsure
Believe in the Vision			
Accept Goals and Challenges			
Positively Impact Culture			

SKILL SET ASSESSMENT FOR INDIVIDUAL PERFORMERS

	Yes	No	Unsure
Produce Results			
Take Necessary Action			
Continuously Improve			

Now that you know what the assessments look like, here's what you're looking for when you use them:

Mindset for leaders

Shared vision: The only way to assess if a leader believes in the vision is to assess if they are sharing that vision on a daily basis. Are they doing so? Do they regularly check in with their team about the organization's vision and how the team's work connects to it?

Growth-focused: Are they focused on organizational, team, and personal growth? Do they believe in the required growth, understand the effort needed for achievement, and communicate it consistently? Do they create opportunities for employees to receive the training and mentorship necessary for growth to take place?

Support the overall health of the organization: Are they actively promoting a healthy culture internally and externally? Are they role-modeling the behaviors needed for a healthy organization?

Promote complete transparency and clarity on goals: Are their teams completely clear on what is expected of them? Is the leader candid with team members and avoid keeping their team in the dark?

Skill set for leaders

Produce results: Are their teams accomplishing their performance goals?

Communicate effectively: Do they communicate effectively both up and down the organization? Can they tailor their communication style as needed to achieve maximum clarity?

Take action: Do they take appropriate and urgent action when needed?

And that's it! You now have a strong baseline understanding of where a particular leader is at with regard to both mindset and skill set.

For individual performers, the assessment process is nearly identical. Here is what to pay attention to for individuals.

Mindset for individuals

Believe in the vision: Does their attitude reflect full belief in the vision? Do they have a clear understanding of what the vision is to begin with?

Accept their goals and challenges: What attitude are you receiving from them? Are you getting "Yes coach, I am all in!" or are you getting "Who set these goals; this is impossible"? When they encounter challenges or barriers, do they respond by investigating potential solutions or do they throw their hands up and give up?

Positively impact the culture: Do they believe in and contribute to the overall health of the organization? Do they support their team members and are they invested in the success of the organization?

Skill set for individuals

Produce results: Are they hitting their goals or aren't they? How consistent is their performance?

Take all necessary actions needed for success: Are they taking action or not? Do they take action in a timely fashion or do they wait until the last minute (or when it's too late)?

Continuously improve: Do they improve when coached and do they take additional self-directed steps to improve their performance?

Your action plan based on the results of each assessment is quite simple. If yes is checked, keep it going! If no is checked, put together an improvement plan. If unsure is checked, spend the time to figure it out.

Now that you know what you are evaluating let's look at the best practices for implementing these assessments.

How and when should you use this

When: The answer is: as often as necessary, but at least once a month.

Things change; mindset is attitude, and numerous factors can impact attitude. It is so crucial to you and your team's success that you evaluate consistently and on an ongoing basis.

How: Each leader should assess their individual performers once a month. Ask them to also assess themselves and set up a one-on-one to discuss the results. The meeting should be a minimum of 20 minutes but generally no longer than 30 minutes. You want enough time to cover all the salient points without it feeling like an interrogation!

You should also share these evaluations once per quarter at the leadership table with your peers so that they can weigh in and keep you honest.

As leaders, we can sometimes be blinded by the relationships we have with our team members. We may know them personally outside of work and struggle to be candid and objective when assessing their performance. Or, we may have developed a bias toward a team member based on past performance, e.g., "Jane has always been a top performer; I just give her all 'yes' checks without even thinking about it."

Sharing your assessments will hold your biases in check and hold you more accountable to objectivity. Jane might always be a top performer, and she might always hit her numbers, but she also might be a culture-killer. She may be undermining mindsets in conversations and actions with others. You may be oblivious to this, but some of your peers may be aware and can bring it to your attention.

It is very important that the leadership team has the datapoints from all of the assessments. It will allow the team to make more informed strategic decisions that will determine future plans. The assessments will also provide you with an understanding of whether or not you are creating and nurturing a healthy and engaged culture overall.

This 5-minute investment in your people is an absolute must for sustained success. So remember: if you want to be a successful leader, spend the time to understand where your team is at and hold everyone accountable.

OBSTACLES AND RESISTANCE TO WOMEN IN LEADERSHIP

*"Sexism goes so deep that at first it's hard
to see; you think it's just reality."*

—Alix Kates Shulman

I WOULD BE DOING everyone who reads this book a disservice if I didn't have a chapter on what to do when you encounter obstacles and resistance to women being in leadership positions. It's easy to think that nobody in this day and age could possibly object to a powerful woman being recognized for her accomplishments, but alas — the dark ages are remarkably persistent.

According to research done by the Pew Research Center on women in leadership,[19] "4 in 10 Americans believe higher standards for women and lack of readiness by companies to hire women for top positions are major reasons there aren't more women in top leadership roles."

Think about that for a minute — everyday people like you and me recognize that many women are denied leadership positions not because they're less capable, but because the company isn't

---

19   http://www.pewsocialtrends.org/2015/01/14/chapter-3-obstacles-to-fe-
      male-leadership/

prepared to have a woman as a leader. The Good 'Ol Boys Club is alive and well.

The same study found that many sexist and outdated perceptions of women are still going strong. Some of the other reasons that respondents cited for women not being in top business positions included women not being tough enough for business, women not being as good of managers as men, and women having too many family responsibilities to successfully run a major corporation.

I have about eight million reasons why those are inaccurate and completely untrue justifications for women not being suited to leadership roles, and I'm sure you could come up with some choice words on the topic as well. The main takeaway is that we have to know what we're up against.

Leadership positions were never designed with women in mind. Courtesy of our old enemy the patriarchy, men have always been the ones to make the rules and set the standards. We're not just trying to change the system to work for us; in many ways, we're trying to tear the whole thing down and rebuild it in a way that will work for everyone instead of just a select few men.

I've talked about some of the factors[20] that result in women having fewer opportunities to hold leadership roles: sexism, patriarchy, racism, and more. But I haven't necessarily given you any strategies for what to do when you find yourself standing in front of someone who is bluntly telling you that they don't think you're fit to lead purely based on your gender.

---

20   http://www.pewsocialtrends.org/2015/01/14/chapter-3-obstacles-to-fe-male-leadership/

Addressing the dearth of women in leadership has always been met with resistance, but in the last few years after the 2016 election in the US, there has been a dramatic spike in how vocal some of those resistors are. The heightened visibility of the issue has proven beyond a doubt that sexism and misogyny is decidedly not a thing of the past, and we need modern strategies to counter modern resistance.

I want to tell you a story about something that really flipped what I thought I knew about the world on its axis: the day I almost jumped off the massage table.

Anyone who knows me knows that I live for my bi-monthly massages. I will move mountains in my schedule to allow for this sacred time with my favorite therapist. It is my time to decompress, relax, and get my travel-weary neck and shoulders the relief they long for.

All of that changed for me one day several months ago, and the aftermath has changed how I think about resistance. On that sunny late-summer day, I bounced into my massage sanctuary and happily saw Susan, my massage therapist, waiting for me. We exchanged our usual greetings and I hopped on the table.

Susan generally knows when to talk to me and when to just let me enjoy the tranquility. Today, I asked her how she was doing in her quest to become a real estate associate. She told me she was still going through the training and asked what was going on with me.

I excitedly told her that I had just finished the first draft of a book I was writing. She became very excited and told me she wanted to write a book as well. She asked me what I was writing about. I told her that I was writing about Women in Leadership and that the motivation for writing it was my outrage at how few women there are in leadership roles. She asked me what I meant, and I gave her some of the statistics. She silently kneaded my shoulders.

Since I had a captive audience of one, I stayed on my soapbox and continued the conversation by telling her about my favorite chapter: "Negotiating the Gender Pay Gap."

Boom! Her silence was broken and she uttered these words: "I simply don't believe in that." Now, sometimes during a massage my brain becomes a little mushy as it is not used to being in a relaxed state. So I asked her what she meant. She repeated herself: "I don't believe in that."

My blissful relaxation was out the window, and I could feel myself tensing up as I asked her why she wouldn't want to be paid the same amount as the man doing the same exact work in the room next door. She very firmly stated that what I was talking about was killing our society and all the good men were being emasculated because of it.

I am pretty sure that I stopped breathing while I tried to comprehend what she was saying. I was ready to jump right off the table. How did I so drastically misjudge the belief system Susan held? How could any woman not want equal pay for equal work?

I was scrambling for something to say that wouldn't lead to an escalated argument, so I simply asked her to tell me a little more about what she meant. She proceeded to tell me that all the men she knew weren't even trying to get ahead anymore because they no longer felt like providers. She told me what I was saying was wrong, because, "If men aren't the providers, they become depressed, start doing drugs, and feel like a failure."

She continued, "They don't even want to get married today because they feel so inferior, and that is going to destroy America." And… "if I ever made more than my husband, he would leave me."

Having written all about the patriarchy in my book, I understood what she was saying on a theoretical level, but it still felt like our conversation was something out of the 1950s instead of the 21st century.

After I left the massage studio, I told the story to several colleagues who shared my reaction. We all shrugged, and I confess that I stopped seeing Susan (and my neck hates me for it). Her words, however, have stayed with me, and I have come to the conclusion that she is not alone in her thoughts.

I was wrong to assume she held what I deemed were natural beliefs on women's advancement, just as I am wrong to wonder why any informed woman voted for and continues to support Donald Trump. And yes, Susan also told me how much she loved our President during our 90-minute conversation.

After stewing in my thoughts for a few weeks, I eventually came to the realization that my conversation with Susan was not necessarily a reflection of her as an individual; it WAS a reflection of how insidious patriarchy and sexism is in our society.

I mean, think about it: the patriarchy has been so wildly effective that it has women actively choosing to support people who will advocate against their best interests and to support men being paid more for the same work. It blew my mind a little bit to have such a blatant example in my own life, but there are a lot of Susans out there. And, as if that wasn't enough, there are a lot of influential men who reinforce those same ideas using their massive platforms.

Enter Tucker Carlson.[21]

On his Fox News Show *Tucker Carlson Tonight*, Carlson stated that women making more than men is causing a crisis in marriage as well as causing more drug and alcohol abuse that leads to incarceration. OMG! Susan and Tucker belong to the same 1950s cult!

Before my jump-off-the-table experience with Susan, I would have shared the exact same sentiments as some of the Twitter respondents. The best one I read was "Dude, are you drunk right now?"

I believe both Tucker and Susan are dead wrong. What I know now that I didn't realize before hearing them was that there are a whole lot of people out there who I wrongly assumed believed in the advancement of women. We need to understand that so we truly know what we are up against.

Tucker Carlson has a massive following of Susans and other men and women who we need to consider. We can't just shrug off the crazy. We need to develop a strategy to somehow bridge these conflicting beliefs.

I think I'll start by going back to Susan and continuing the dialog. I know that at the very least my neck will be happy. As

---

21   https://www.huffingtonpost.com/entry/tucker-carlson-men-in-decline-fox-news_us_5c2dbc24e4b0407e90881dcc

for my recommendations about what you can try if and when you meet Susans and Tuckers in your own life? Here are a few ideas:

- **Know Your Limits:** Start by getting in the habit of checking in with yourself about how much energy you have to really dive deep with someone spouting sexist opinions. You have no obligation to have a conversation every time you hear something — and sometimes it might even be dangerous for you to try.

If I'm exhausted and hanging on by a thread when I get on the massage table, that might not be the time for me to strike up a dialogue with Susan. Chances are good; I'll snap or say something I'll regret later, and the conversation will go nowhere.

Conversely, if I jump on the table and feel grounded and in a good headspace, I'm more likely to be able to listen to Susan and have genuine dialogue with her.

- **Pick Your Battles:** The sad reality is that there are people out there who are never going to change their minds. You could talk until you're blue in the face and they'll still wholeheartedly believe that women are naturally inferior to men and don't deserve to be in leadership positions. Those are not the people you want to pour your energy into!

  If there are people you know who hold opposing views to your own but seem open to a dialogue, you'll likely have much better luck talking with them to understand their points and try to help them understand where you're coming from too.

- **Assess Your Sphere of Influence:** Think about the people you interact with on a daily basis: co-workers, friends, family, roommates, spouses or partners, etc. These are the people who are more likely to be receptive to hearing about your perspective on things and sharing their thoughts with you.

  Tucker Carlson would probably never even see a tweet I made in response to his show, but the high-school girls I coach? They're going to be way more likely to listen when I say that women deserve to be paid equally and that women are just as capable as men of leading.

- **Don't Try to Change People's Minds:** This is one of the hardest things for me. My natural inclination is to go in and start listing off statistics and citing stories and news reports about the damage that patriarchy and sexism cause women. But honestly? All that's likely going to do is make whomever I'm talking to feel defensive and like they have to stick to their guns or they'll look stupid.

In this day and age where even our president dismisses news he doesn't personally like as "fake news," it's all too easy for people to ignore what you're saying or write it off as being biased. Instead of trying to change people's minds, think about it in terms of trying to understand where they're coming from while sharing your own views. Remember that earlier chapter on communication and dialogue vs. debate? Yeah, we're going for dialogue here (tempting though debate may be).

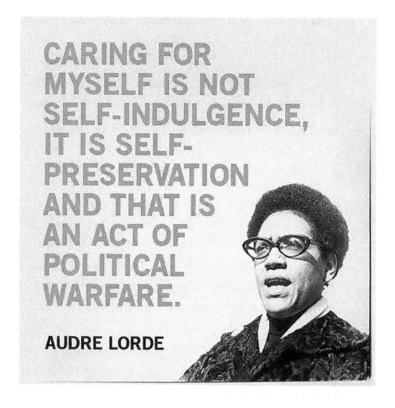

CARING FOR MYSELF IS NOT SELF-INDULGENCE, IT IS SELF-PRESERVATION AND THAT IS AN ACT OF POLITICAL WARFARE.

AUDRE LORDE

If I openly talk about my experiences as a woman in leadership positions with Susan and also listen with an open mind to what she has to say, maybe at some point she'll think to herself, "Huh, you know what? That Shelley said something the other day that kind of makes sense, even though it's different from what I was taught to believe. Maybe there's something to it after all."

Trying to create change and push back against resistance this way is a long process, and it can be exhausting to try to talk with people who are questioning your humanity and worth. If you're going to have these kinds of dialogues, make sure you're taking care of yourself so you don't get burned out.

- **Cultivate a Supportive Circle:** This could be friends, co-workers, family — whoever you want it to be. The important thing is that you have some people you can turn to when the proverbial shit hits the fan and you can't handle one more minute of patriarchal nonsense.

  This circle of people will be your lifeline when you encounter resistance and obstacles in your path; they can help you brainstorm strategies, listen to you vent about how messed up it is that we still have to have these conversations, and drink wine (or your beverage of choice) with you when you've had one of *those* days.

  They're your safe harbor in the storm, and you'll be able to return the favor to others who are trying to conquer the opposition to women's leadership once and for all!

Again, creating this kind of change is a long-term effort. In the Pew Research study I referenced at the beginning of this chapter, they found that over half of Americans don't believe that women will achieve parity with men in top executive business positions in the foreseeable future.

It can feel disheartening not to see immediate change, and even to think that we might not see true parity in our lifetimes, but remember: change IS possible. Think about how far we've come in the last century.

In the United States, we've gone from women being systematically denied education, being unable to vote, and being treated as property to women having PhDs, seeing a massive surge in the number of women elected to public office in the 2018 elections, and having countless role models we can look to for examples of strong women leaders.

That's a remarkable amount of progress in a relatively short time frame, and it would never have happened with persistent resistance. We aren't just working on creating equity for ourselves; we're building a different world for the generations of women and girls who come after us.

If you need a little additional inspiration, check out the song Hands Dirty by the band Delta Rae.[22] It's pretty much the perfect anthem for women who are working to dismantle oppressive systems and achieve equity (and it's dang catchy, too!)

While we keep working for change, continue striving to make your leadership aspirations a reality. Conquering this crisis of inequity is as timely as ever, and every day spent in the trenches makes a difference. I hope that this book has given you new tools and tactics to use in your journey to the top, and I wish you the best in your leadership adventure!

---

22   https://www.youtube.com/watch?v=nLP3-6C_Egw

WANT MORE?

Do you want leadership coaching? Go to https://dunagangroup.com/executive-coaching/

Want to attend one of our FOUR "Dig Deeper" Leadership Accelerator workshops in 2019? Go to https://dunagangroup.com/2019-dig-deeper-leadership-accelerators/

Need help in recruiting top female leaders? Go to https://dunagangroup.com/talent-solutions/

CPSIA information can be obtained
at www.ICGtesting.com
Printed in the USA
LVHW041024110319
610188LV00014B/176/P